JOURNEY IN PROGRESS

SELECTED POEMS:
CAROLINE REEVES

PHOTOGRAPHS:
ALLAN REEVES
&
CAROLINE REEVES

REDHAWK
PUBLICATIONS

Journey In Progress Copyright ©2021 Caroline Reeves and Allan Reeves

Published by Redhawk Publications
            2550 US Hwy 70 SE
            Hickory, NC 28602

Robert Canipe, Publisher and General Editor
Tim Peeler, Editor
Patty Thompson, Project and Permissions Coordinator

ISBN:

Printed in the United States of America

To

Joseph,

Alexander,

Michael,

David,

And

Timothy,

Thank you, as always, for everything.

Table of Contents

Khan El-Khalil Market, Cairo 9

A World within a World 12

Kizhi Island, Russia 16

Cupidity 21

Quinta da Boa Vista, Rio 24

Cornflower Blue Morning 29

Cow Crossing in Rajasthan 34

Gentlewomen Farmers 38

Camel Ride in Giza 43

Graduation from West Point 48

Acuario Valparaiso 53

Entrapped 57

Summer Bugs 63

Arrival in Roma 66

Thanksgiving Parade in Philadelphia 71

Sunset at Luxor Temple 77

Consequences 79

Mass at Basilica de la Merced 83

Twenty Miles a Day 87

Great Wall of China 91

Ladies' Lunch 95

Colosseum 99

"Uno, Por Favor" 103

Riots in Santiago 107

Crossroads 111

Exodus from Gambia 115

Family Vacation 119

Harvest 123

Terracotta Warriors, X'ian 127

The Much-Anticipated Play 131

Cross Country 135

Rose 139

La Serenissma- Un Anno a Venezia 143

About the Authors 147

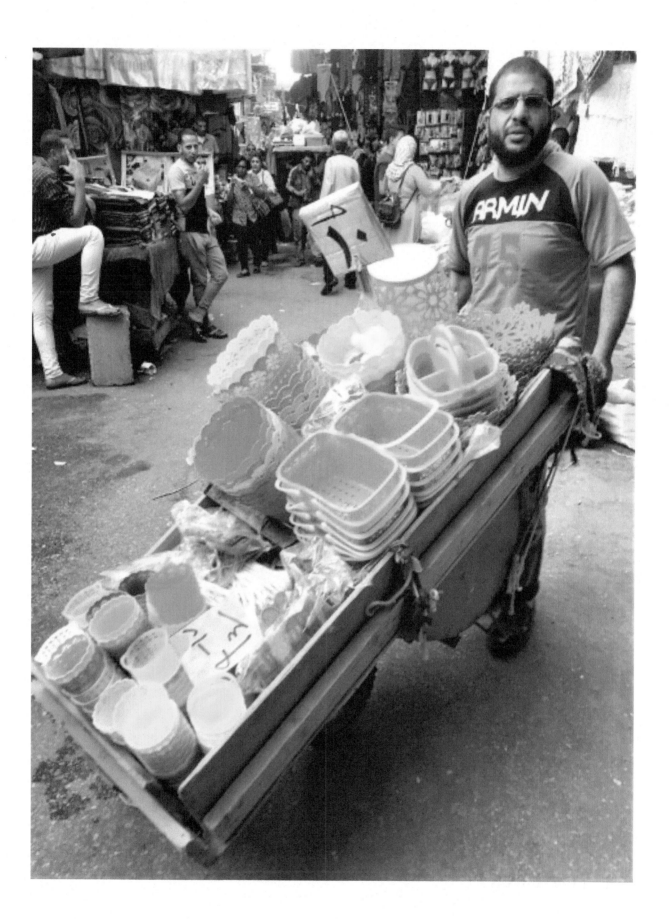

1. Khan El-Khalil Market, Cairo

Our eyes meet…

Yours questioning,

Projecting intimations of beauty,

From behind the narrow slits of your burka.

Our eyes meet…

Yours pleading,

Teenage melancholy and ennui,

A turbulent and restive visage.

Our eyes meet…

Yours decidedly annoyed,

Balancing plastic neon pails on a wooden cart,

I am in your way.

Our eyes meet…

Some gentle, some curious,

Some incensed by my audacity,

Clicking away at my cell phone.

Kaleidoscopic scarves,

Mortar and pestles,

Roasted corn on a stick,

Cumin and coriander,

Marjoram and wisteria,

Hedged in wicker baskets

Balanced evenly on donkey spines.

Our eyes meet…

As I hand over coins for spices,

Touching the leathery palm of your hand,

The crisp and pungent scent of jasmine,

Stirring and confirming,

Our intimate, yet transcendent, connection.

2. World within a World

The large television mounted on the wall

Blares reruns of *Modern Family*,

While residents sit,

Perched in wheelchairs,

Blindly staring at the wall,

Or the space in between.

Parents whose children

Never forgave them for their sins,

Spinsters who never had children

to never forgive them for their sins,

Left alone with nurse's aides,

Unskilled and underpaid,

The stench of urine eschewing visitors,

Who chose to forget,

Or seek not to be reminded of

The world within a world.

A new episode of *Modern Family*

Erupts on the screen,

While trays of pureed chicken and turnips

Are perfunctorily distributed,

Hooked with special devices

Onto the armrests of wheelchairs.

It is more convenient

To feed the residents

In the "Entertainment Room,"

Where they can be easily toileted

In the large adjoining bathroom

While continuing to enjoy the show.

Mrs. McGillicuty,

The newest occupant,

Who has not yet surrendered to gloom,

Perspicaciously compares her surroundings

To a time long-past,

When old age was venerable,

And wisdom was imparted by grandparents,

Surrounding a dining room table with family,

Eating roast beef and Yorkshire pudding,

The smell of good food and laughter,

Delighting the appetites

Of young and old.

After toileting,

Residents are corralled to their rooms,

Changed into night gowns and diapers,

And loaded onto beds,

A routine which would replay

Every single afternoon.

Blackout curtains are drawn,

Simulating darkness,

And nighttime,

Inviting sleep,

Dreams,

And a temporary escape,

From the world within a world.

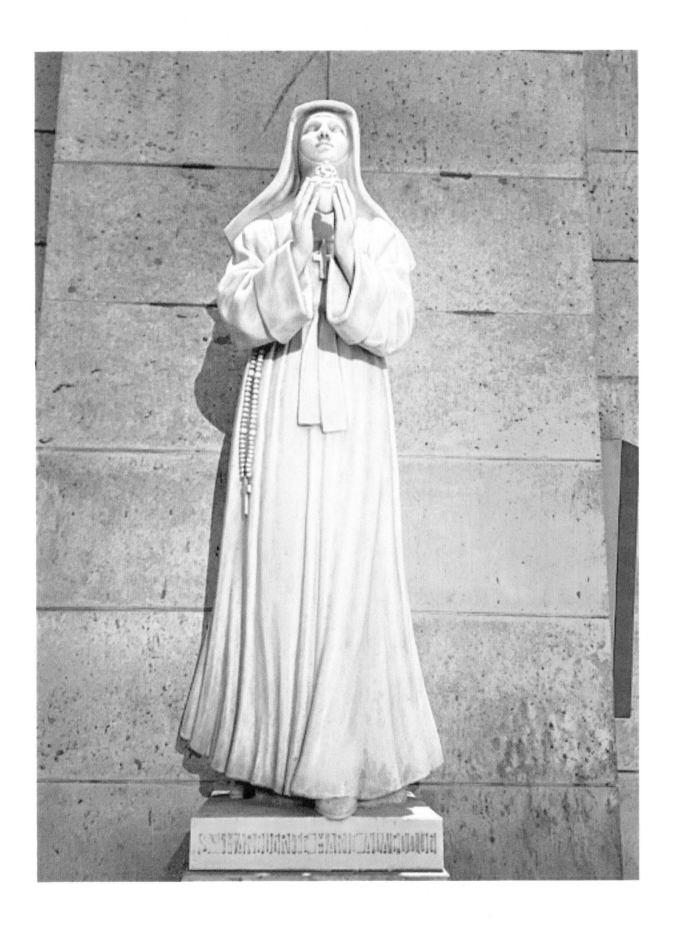

3. Kizhi Island, Russia

The morning air is bracing

As the hydrofoil speeds along Lake Onega

On route to Kizhi Island.

Shivering, he wraps a heavy wool blanket

Around his shoulders,

Its rough texture as irritating as

His ersatz burlap tunic.

Upon arrival, he is allowed

One cup of strong, bitter coffee,

And a slice of yesterday's stale bread

Before taking his station,

A coveted job for a man with only

Two fingers and a stump on his right hand,

A casualty of a scything accident

Before farming was banned in '71.

"All for the better" he thinks to himself.

When the tourists convene,

After the sun has risen,

They stare curiously at his remaining digits

As he feigns the role of 17th century woodworker,

Sawing and sanding,

A collection of children's toys,

While husbanding the rubles

Offered for purchase.

It is September,

And soon the island,

As an open-air museum,

Will be closed for winter,

And he will be unemployed.

The tourists' chatter rankles him

As he ponders his predicament,

Calculating how many potatoes and carrots

He can stow away over the months to come.

Sequestered in thought,

A leonine woman nudges him,

Holding out a 1000 ruble bill,

"No toy today" she signals,

Releasing the bill tenderly

In his mangled hand,

Both swathed by the steeples

Of the towering,

Yet decaying,

Church of the Transfiguration.

4. Cupidity

The inculcations of his frugal German mother,

"Genug ist zu viel"

Enough is too much,

Never carried much weight

Because enough was never enough.

No amount of Bulgari watches, Armani suits, Hermes ties,

Porsches, Aston Martins, Bentleys,

Chalets, penthouses, villas or skyscrapers

Could satisfy his rapacious appetite,

Quench his avaricious thirst,

Or placate his insurmountable quest

To accumulate more and more and more.

The teachings of evolved beings,

Like Gandhi or Mother Theresa,

To live in the present,

Radiating strength and wisdom,

From inner abundance,

Were useless to him.

Because the present was irrelevant.

He lived only in the future.

Scheming a daily, monthly, yearly, lifelong,

Bifurcated mission

To amass more money

And then figure out how to spend it

Because enough was never,

And would never be,

Enough.

5. Quinta da Boa Vista, Rio

The Museu Nacional,

Fenced in and boarded up,

A skeleton of the past,

Former palace of kings and queens,

Relegated to a dilapidated and graffitied structure

Housing dinosaur fossils,

Sabre-toothed tiger remains,

Pre-Columbian relics,

Only, eventually,

To be almost completely destroyed by fire.

Millions of reals worth of taxidermy,

Stuffed birds, mammals and fish,

Obliterated in one sweeping blaze,

A habitat's history extinguished.

No attempt at renovation,

Although a sign indicates

"Work in Progress."

I see no work or progress.

We proceed in the drizzling rain,

Sharing one undersized travel umbrella,

Down a long path lined with healthy royal palms,

Past children playing in grottoes,

Skewered with more graffiti,

Towards the Jardim Zoologico,

"Home to thousands of reptiles, birds and mammals,"

Indigenous to Brazil,

And its striated landscape.

The zoo is also under construction,

And fenced off,

But we are granted passage

At half price admission,

To view a limited selection,

"birds, small monkeys, and hippopotamuses."

Large cages provide the abode

For myriad birds who can only fly,

At most, a few wing flaps,

Scarlet and Hyacinth Macaws,

Toco Toucans and Burrowing Owls,

All doomed for imprisonment,

Never again to fully spread their wing span,

And soar across the open azure skies.

We move on to the small monkey cages

Where Marmosets, Tamarins, and Howlers

Pace back and forth

In a crazed methodical pattern

Only to stop occasionally

To make eye contact with the visitor,

Pleading for an escape,

As their little hands

Shake the wire mesh.

The task of observing the hippopotamuses

Still remains,

But I have had enough,

And the rain has begun to fall harder,

Heedlessly pelting weighty droplets,

From a gray, cloud-saturated sky,

Offering no hint of prescient sunlight.

6. Cornflower Blue Morning

Cornflower blue sky,

Unencumbered with clouds,

Picture perfect autumn morning,

Slight breeze, low humidity,

Comforting sun,

Caressing one's every move,

Children happily at school,

The excitement of a new year

Fresh on their rosy cheeks.

I am early to work

Sitting at my desk,

Warming up my computer,

When a colleague darts in,

"A plane has crashed into the twin towers"

He announces urgently.

My computer continues to rumble,

As I stare at the blank screen.

Waiting, I think to myself,

"Probably a commuter plane with engine trouble,"

Until imminently my colleague darts in again,

Obstreperously trumpeting

"Another plane just hit the second tower!"

I pound urgently on the enter key of my computer,

Until finally the screen erupts with the announcement

"Planes Crash into Twin Towers!"

News I already know.

A few moments later,

Broadcast of planes shattering the pentagon

And Schwenksville spills from my computer,

And the mouths of my co-workers.

"America under attack!" I see on the screen,

And then everything shuts down,

Dead, blank, nothing.

My computer has also crashed.

I stare at the blackness not knowing what to do.

After an hour or so,

We are told to go home.

The office is closed.

I walk hurriedly to the train station,

Folding into the chaos

Of a hapless and desperate flock,

Likewise dismissed early from work.

I look up at the tall buildings as I traverse 16th St.,

Thinking of how I will seek coverage when another plane hits.

"Philadelphia is next!"

I hear someone bellow,

As we push and shove our way,

Seeking order in the desultory

Machinations of the panicked crowd.

When I journey underground to get my train,

Everyone again is pushing and shoving,

The car is packed in a way I have never

Seen before, lacking the order of a conductor.

I try to thrust my way inside,

Putting one foot onto the slip-resistant pad,

As if that would claim a space,

But the doors begin to close,

And I am left out,

On the platform,

With my harried compatriots,

Again proclaiming

"Philadelphia is next!"

I get choked up,

Thinking about my kids,

And that I may never see them again,

I've heard that this is what everyone thinks,

In times like these,

An inevitable and painfully veritable cliché.

Another train arrives shortly,

It is evident they are corralling us out of the city.

When I arrive back in the suburbs,

I head immediately to the elementary school,

Where heart strung parents are gathering their children,

Scooping them from classrooms and playgrounds,

Transporting them to the insulation,

Of family homesteads,

A callow attempt

At seeking refuge from

And defending against

the pernicious attack on

the cornflower blue morning.

7. Cow Crossing in Rajasthan

Bovine wanderers,

Hundreds,

Roam freely,

Peacefully unfettered,

Tan, beige, brown,

Spotted and flecked,

Ribs jutting prominently,

Beneath withers,

Sleek and lustrous.

We fold into the sacred sea,

Offering stalks of grass

To the gentle masses,

Our car en route to

Amber Palace in Jaipur,

Temporarily suspended

By the peregrinations

Of serene and soulfully

Unencumbered creatures.

8. Gentlewomen Farmers

We spray the fruit trees

With anti-insecticide,

Attempting to aim the nozzle,

Down-wind.

"Mom, is this stuff toxic?"

"I don't think so."

Not so reassuring,

I ponder

As I inhale a delicate sprinkling

Of pesticides.

"I hope we have a good apple crop this year."

Concords grapes, a pear tree,

Gooseberry and raspberry bushes,

An abundant buffet,

Already meticulously attended to,

By a thriving deer population

Who will be undeterred

by the delicate mist of chemicals.

It is late in the afternoon

And I am as tired from farm work,

As you are indefatigable,

Your eighty-five-year-old body,

More resilient than mine has ever been.

We are on a quest

Of bug annihilation.

I haul the sprayer can

And magic wand of death

Pumping it every few minutes

To gain the yardage and force

To reach the very tip

Of the treasured walnut tree.

"Anything else?" I inquire

With a conclusory tone.

"There is a sour cherry tree

Way in the back of the field."

I sigh internally

And lug my obliteration hardware

Across a mess of overgrown weeds

And menacing blackberry thorns,

Scraping my bare legs,

And drawing a trail of blood droplets

Demarking my march of death.

The ground is uneven and muddy,

The mosquitos rampant and voracious,

Another blood fest,

To add to the tour of duty.

When we are finally finished,

We sit back in worn Adirondack chairs,

Sipping sugary lemon iced tea,

Two gentlewomen farmers,

Celebrating,

a hard-fought crusade

Of pest eradication.

9. Camel Ride in Giza

The gentle pulse of his hooves

Treading softly through the sand

Past the Khufu pyramid

Giza's tallest at 750 feet,

Even more massive

From the perspective

Of a seven foot Dromedary,

She clutches the reins firmly

As his coarse shaggy fur

ripples in the breeze.

He raises his long neck,

Prominent incisors reflecting the sun,

As they pass the Khafre pyramid.

Is this his favorite?

She wonders.

The middle pyramid.

Something balanced,

And unassuming,

If possible, in a 470 foot structure.

He picks up pace

As they pass the Menkaure pyramid

Saddle wavering tenuously on uneven turf,

His long eyelashes batting wind-blown sand,

Large nostrils flailing.

"Whoa, whoa!"

She commands,

As if he would understand.

Remarkably,

He slows,

His leathery patched knees,

Again, regulating his pace.
She reaches forward
With one arm
Petting the back of his neck,
Almost touching his little ear,
"Good camel"
She whispers softly
"Good camel."

10. Graduation from West Point

Metered motion,

Frame by frame,

Like an old movie,

Fluttering through the projector,

She, watches him,

Step by step,

Striding to the stage.

When his name is announced,

The name she gave him,

The day he was born,

Twenty-two years ago,

He glides regally to the podium,

Impeccable posture,

In his dress uniform.

Freeze frame…Stop…Hold…Pause…

Black and white negatives…

Sunlight…

Shadows…

Adumbrations of the future.

Cool sobering breeze,

He shakes the President's hand,

Accepting his diploma,

Confidently,

Emphatically,

Without reservation.

Proud parents cheer loudly and sob softly

As 1000 more cadets become officers,

Babies, little boys and girls, adolescents,

Who grew up way too quickly.

When the name of the "goat" is called,

The corps cheers exuberantly,

The lowest ranked in the class

Is now an officer too.

Reception Day, Acceptance Day,

Affirmation Oath, Ring Weekend,

Parades, gala's and ubiquitous football games,

The past four years flash by…

Freeze frame…Stop…Hold…Pause…

Dizzyingly unable to cling to the past,

Or even embrace the present,

She thinks of the future,

As if propelling a grenade

Directly at conjured equanimity,

A self-inflicted wound

Of her own making.

After officer training,

Her son will be deployed,

Perhaps to Iraq, Afghanistan or Syria,…

He will be put "in harm's way,"

A very stale euphemism for

"Die a violent and painful death."

The brutal, underlying fact,

Of life at West Point

That no amount of military pageantry

Can gloss over,

The insidious elephant in the room,

Inexorable and unyielding.

After the last diploma is handed out,

The First Captain of the corps

Roars commandingly into the microphone

"Claaaass Dismissed!"

The stadium erupts into deafening applause,

Standing, jumping, cheering, jostling,

While hats fly into the air,

As little children are released onto the field,

To capture descending mementos of the ceremony.

Tears flow freely from parents' eyes,

Few attempting to veil their emotions,

As visions of the past, present and future,

Converge for one fleeting,

Euphoric, confusing,

And staggeringly overwhelming,

Moment in time.

11. Acuario Valparaiso- Un Mundo a Explorar

At 7,000 pesos,

There are no other patrons,

Just us,

And the fish,

And a few eels.

The cashier,

Appears almost conspiratorial,

As we sheepishly offer admission funds.

The aquarium,

Once envisioned

As the pride of Valparaiso,

Regally overlooks

The South Pacific Ocean.

Upon entering there is a children's room,

With a diminutive table covered with crayons,

And pages ripped out from a fish coloring book,

But no children,

Only me,

As I scuttle into a small chair,

Observing the lifeless surroundings.

On the second floor,

A "touch-me" tank offers

Visitors, "young and old,"

The opportunity to submerge hands

Into an icy cistern

To stroke the backs

Of mini-stingrays

As they sashay between

Collections of faux coral reefs.

Assuming they are not venomous,

I dip my hand into the frigid sea kingdom,

And gingerly palpate

A slimy pectoral fin.

Enough fun here,

I pump a generous helping

Of hand sanitizer

And move on to the next exhibit,

The crown jewel,

A big fish tank,

Imbedded in the center of

A darkened room.

Mesmerized,

By a neon yellow swimmer,

I hone my nascent aqua-photography skills,

Following him back and forth,

From one end of the vivarium,

To the other,

Endless,

Pointless motion,

Mindless, mechanical repetition,

In a murky pool of obscurity.

12. Entrapped

"Today will be the day I am set free"

The mantra which sustains you.

Gone are the days of lavish dinners,

Peking Duck at Dadong,

Caviar blini's at Mu Si Ke,

And Hot Pot prepared exclusively by your chef,

Bubbling in a large caldron on the dining room table.

Your vineyard in Macedonia,

Is probably shriveling by now,

As is your body in the cell.

"Who ratted me out?"

A question which compels negativity

When you are trying to stay positive.

The delicate saffron smell of your wife's alabaster skin,

Brushing against her silk muu muu dress

Breathing in the memory almost resuscitates,

Reinvigorates, enlivens the dank mildew odor

Which emanates from your creaky iron bed

And decades old sweat stained mattress.

"Who ratted me out?"

The negativity creeps back in.

"Was it my driver?"

"The cement contractor for Sun Hao Complex?"

"My first wife?"

The questions erode your mind.

They came that night,

While you were sleeping soundly

After a night of Moutai wine and Gambai toasts,

Dragging you from your bed, nude,

As your wife and young son huddled,

Clinging to each other in terror

In the far corner of the milky room,

Its comfort shattered irreparably.

Day number 628.

And counting.

"Today will be the day I am set free"

You repeat the mantra,

Attempting to dispel negativity,

Manufacture optimism.

Relations with the guards are good,

As your lawyer has plied them with smoked meats

And champagne on a regular basis.

Likewise, relations with fellow inmates are good,

As your lawyer has supplied delicacies,

Which you share,

The kind many have never eaten before,

Foie Gras on toast points with Indonesian capers.

Yet,

There is no trial.

No formal charges.

No evidence.

Only the insular breed of justice meted out

In a curiously vapid and ignominious scenario.

They took the money from the safe that night.

Millions, if not billions, of RMB's.

The count varied on a daily basis,

As you, a businessman, earned and expended,

Extravagantly and indulgently.

It is all gone now.

"Who gave them the combination?"

This question gnaws at you the most.

"Was it the guy who sold me the safe?"

"My mistress?"

"Her mother?"

"My brother?"

You shake the paranoia like an irksome insect.

Reality is too painful to address

As you lay supine on your smelly cot.

These were not bribes,

Only incentives.

This is the way we do business here,

You reassure yourself

Trumpeting your hollow defense

In a world encapsulated by injustice.

"Today will be the day I am set free"

13. Summer Bugs

The insect population appears to multiply during summer

Or is it just that the days are longer

And there is more time to discern their presence.

Unable to coexist peacefully,

I wage war on a daily basis.

Combat starts in the shower in the morning with

Something that looks like a long-legged mosquito,

But slower and less menacing,

I curse with bellicosity as I smush it with my hand and

Wash the hapless creature down the drain.

Next battle involves a moth fluttering about teasingly as I towel off,

Followed by a series of flies in the kitchen

Circling my coffee cup.

On my drive to work a massive hairy spider ascends from out of nowhere

Onto my dash board,

I spray it with hand sanitizer

While trying not to veer off of the highway.

My son, who studies etymology, reminds me that there are

Three times the number of bugs than all other animals combined,

Pollinators, food sources, silk and shellac makers,

not only dominating but sustaining our ecosystem.

I once read that Marilyn Monroe so hated to kill insects,

That she would gingerly transport them out of her house in a Kleenex.

I, the curmudgeon in the shower,

And spider killer in the minivan,

Have not yet reached that level

Of enlightenment.

14. Arrival in Roma

Via Maggiore,

A lengthy trek from Termini station,

With luggage,

On wheels,

Navigating cobblestone streets,

And narrow sidewalks,

Our GPS irresolutely leading the way.

Arriving downtrodden at our destination,

Hotel Donatella,

An elderly man and his wife,

With exquisitely polished fuchsia nails,

Welcome us,

With hearty handshakes

And glasses of Limoncello.

We sit and sip our drinks,

At ten in the morning,

On well-worn leather sofas,

In the rustic lobby while

The cameriera readies our room.

Signora promptly joins our cabal,

Unleashing a variegated city map,

With blazing elan,

 Fervently circling piazza after piazza,

While gushing a dizzying

Amalgamation of Italian and English,

Highlighted with prolific gesticulation.

As Signora ardently circles,

Signore approaches,

Commanding a battle charge

With the authority of a four-star General,

Well-seasoned in the art of cartography,

"Ristorante! Mangia Bene, Vivi Felice!"

He imperiously pens large inky X's

On the positions of culinary institutions

We are to conquer on our mission.

With marching orders in place,

Reconnaissance map in hand,

And jet lag transciently vanquished

By visions of ossobuco and carbonara,

We advance back to Via Maggiore,

Emboldened with a new sense

Of courage, audacity and self-determination.

15. Thanksgiving Parade in Philadelphia

Festooning Benjamin Franklin Parkway,

Flags of 195 nations,

Conga tempestuously with the squalls,

Vestiges of forefathers' dreams.

A high school marching band

Plays *Hallelujah* as

Crowds beetle between

Syrupy fried waffle stands and

Impresarios hawking dollar water bottles

From iced shopping carts.

The flag of Lebanon,

Displaying the aegis of a solitary pine tree,

Undulates recalcitrantly against violent gusts,

Having sidelined the balloons,

A scheduled omission

Bringing heartache

To crestfallen masses.

The crowd,

Decisively homogenous,

Casts shadow,

On the *City of Brotherly Love.*

Sporadic revelers embrace a man,

Holding a *Free Hugs* sign,

The scent of his cologne,

Like lilies of the valley,

On a spring day,

Providing an evanescent reprieve,

As flags of Liberia and Lithuania,

(mounted alphabetically),

Billow querulously in the wind.

16. Sunset at Luxor Temple

Massive imposing columns,

Some over eighty feet tall,

Mimicking bountiful papyrus stalks,

Hypostyle Hall,

The divine mansion.

Etchings of tall straight-backed Egyptians,

Ducks, horses, falcons and ostriches,

Conducting lives in seamless harmony.

Adidas sneakers and Birkenstock sandals,

Dwarfed by the artful longevity,

Shuffle along sandy walks,

Highlighting temporal incongruity.

Sanctuary of the past,

Denoting a time

As simple and orderly,

As the Hieroglyphics engraved,

On the temple walls.

Inhaling the scent of bygone eras,

As the setting sun,

illuminates an impression,

Of a man on a chariot,

Readying his bow and arrow,

To slaughter,

A cowering,

Mid-sized creature,

Dinner for the family,

Three thousand years ago.

The moon's silver slipper

Ascends knowingly into

The twilight blue sky.

Offering a reverential salutation,

To towering effigies of Ramsus II,

A perennial landscape,

Solid and lasting,

Poised and unperturbable,

Piqued only,

Very slightly,

By the steadfast rhythm,

Of the Nile's luxuriously tempered,

Waves of antiquity.

17. Consequences

Gingerly sipping his morning coffee,

Ethiopian blend with steamed almond milk,

He triumphantly confirms the NBA lineup,

Perusing the screen of his computer.

This has been a good year.

News flash to the side:

Students in Hong Kong Protesting Mainland's Policies,

Police Interpose with Tear Gas and Rubber Bullets.

Instantly,

He is reminded of his college days,

Youthful exuberance,

Protesting injustices.

Inspired by the nascent courage,

Across the globe,

Across the decades,

He sends a tweet,

To his many followers,

Supporting the young protesters.

Freedom of speech,

To him,

Like a reflex of the knee

Summoned by the swift tap

Of a doctor's mallet.

Within minutes,

A call from the Commissioner

Pierces his cellphone.

Party leaders,

Irate with his message,

Have cancelled the NBA tournament in China.

No further games to be scheduled.

Multitudes will be unemployed.

Players will suffer.

Fans will suffer.

And the economy will most certainly suffer.

He fears he will also lose his job.

International coalescence ripped

By one thoughtful,

Or thoughtless tweet.

Justice has been swift and truculent,

Extirpating and annihilating,

First Amendment rights,

Which,

Until now,

Flowed as smoothly and naturally,

As the rich, red blood in his veins.

18. Mass at Basilica de la Merced

Fiestas Patrias,

Chile's Independence Day,

Most businesses closed,

Except churches and restaurants,

Sustenance providers.

Basilica de la Merced,

Filled to capacity,

With an avid crowd,

Seeking spiritual pabulum.

Following Signos de Paz

And Padre Nuestro,

Many traverse the center aisle,

Arriving at the altar,

To receive hosts,

Unswervingly on their tongues,

While others remain in pews,

Contemplating past, present and future.

El sacerdote then processes,

Up, down, sideways,

Sprinkling holy water,

From an ancient aspergillum,

A sign that all is cleansed,

And forgiven,

Incense and hymns,

Blanketing the moment

Like the soft embrace

Of a gentle woman's arms.

19. Twenty Miles a Day

Tired, hot, filthy, feet

Covered with blisters, callouses,

Cracked skin with bleeding crevasses,

Inhabiting cheap shoes,

Flip flops or plastic sandals,

Your instruments of transportation,

To a place,

Where no one welcomes you,

Loves you,

Cares about you,

And at times actively hates you.

It is your dream that

A new dawn might bring

A basin of warm soapy water

To wash your battered feet,

A fresh towel to dry them,

Clean white cotton socks,

Adidas running shoes,

With arch support,

A friendly smile,

A compassionate hug,

Arms stretched wide open,

Welcoming you home,

After a long journey.

20. Great Wall of China

Dissecting the northern border,

A colossal edifice,

Redoubtable presence,

Incongruous with the serenity

Of a sunny October afternoon.

Subjugation, regulation, asphyxiation,

Inspirations for construction,

Maniacally erected,

Over thousands of years,

Sacrificing hundreds of thousands of lives,

Ultimately proving obscenely otiose.

A steep climb to the top lookout tower,

Overcrowded with blissful tourists,

Celebrating the ascent,

Rewards with sweeping views

Of the Mutianyu mountains,

Nuanced with mint green and amber hues,

Distinct reminders

Of the wall's gradual metamorphosis,

From a tool of divisiveness,

Into a bastion of smooth and silky coalescence.

Magnetism, attraction, defiance,

Visible easily from a plane's descent,

Unincumbered and radiant,

Carved and succinct,

Pouring leisurely into

The muted glance of

An unsuspecting eye.

21. Ladies' Lunch

"Let's go have a milkshake" you trumpet zestfully.

I agree, even though I am not in the mood for one.

You bring four dogs on four colorful leashes for our milkshake walk,

The big shaggy poodle keeps trying to hump me and the other dogs.

I ask if I can bring my dog and you say your dogs are not friendly.

I didn't even know you liked dogs.

You tell me it's a new dog walking job.

What a multitasker you are with me, the milkshake and the dogs.

After a brief walk down the avenue, we arrive at a stately,

Pale yellow mansion that has been converted into a restaurant.

There has been a change of plans, the milkshake has turned into lunch.

Two other friends join us in the vestibule.

There are no tables available.

We peer down into the dining room

Where conversant patrons are sipping petite flutes of sherry,

Gazing across tables adorned with pale pink peonies,

While nibbling watercress and creamed cheese tea sandwiches.

We put our name on a waiting list

And go into the kitchen to wait.

I'm not sure what you did with the dogs.

We sit at a couple of concrete slabs with the kitchen staff.

It is steamy and poorly ventilated.

You smoke two cigarettes quickly with one of the other friends,

Who apparently is a smoker who is trying to quit.

I attempt futilely to make small talk,

Asking the non-smoker friend about her golf game.

She plays several times a week and has an impressive handicap.

I tell her that I purchased golf clubs at a garage sale,

And have gone to a driving range.

She is unimpressed.

The friends say they have been here before,

And were always able to score a good table.

Maybe it is me or the dogs.

We continue to wait in the muggy kitchen.

Eventually, the hostess resurfaces.

She relays news that a table is available,

However, not in the main dining room with the sherry and peonies.

Following her lead,

We trudge through long corridors with towering stone sculptures and

White crown molding adorning pastel colored walls.

You tell me you tied the dogs up in the foyer.

When we arrive at our destination,

It is in a cramped side room,

With noisy children and greasy industrial tables.

We order food, hot heavy goulashes,

Clearly at odds with the tea sandwiches,

And muted hue of the rest of the mansion.

You order a side of lobster to compensate.

When the waiter brings the check,

I insist on paying for my own meal,

Contributing way more than my share.

As we depart, finally, we again pass the clients in the main dining room

Engulfed in the glory of its splendor,

Oblivious to our gawking.

The friends comment

That it's a much better experience

In the main dining room.

I unleash the dogs

And look for a bowl of water.

22. Colosseum

Painstakingly long lines,

Wrapping halfway around the monument,

Welcome tourists, as the unforgiving sun

Beats down on the pavement.

Overheated and dehydrated,

We buy a cool bottle of water

From a wandering salesman,

Our thirst joyously quenched

And spirits now assuaged

By the memory of morning mass

At San Giovanni de Laterano,

With its scent of liturgical incense

And echo of Gregorian chants.

Eventually,

After two hours,

And two security clearances,

We are granted access.

Ascending a narrow stone stairwell,

Onto the second floor of the arena,

We channel hapless beings,

Criminals, slaves, and insurrectionists,

Lions, giraffes, and elephants.

Doors of Death dot the landscape.

Animals emerging suddenly,

Through a hatch,

Onto the stage,

Added drama to the performance.

Audience participation,

Clamors and combustions,

Could signal life or death,

While adorning the Emperor

In a cloak of compassion or

Blanket of savagery.

Ultimately, death could be drawn out,

Providing maximum theatrics

For the price of one admission ticket.

A festive barbeque on the lawn,

(Also included with the admission ticket)

Would invariably follow,

Roasting unfortunate creatures,

Who had met their demise,

Appetites whetted

By sport and bloodshed.

Heading back to our hotel,

After a day of imagined theatrics,

We stumble upon a modest basilica,

Where a baby is being baptized,

Coddled by adoring relatives,

Her diminutive body

Bathed in sunlight

As water trickles gently

Down the sides of

Her delicate alabaster face.

23. "Uno, Por Favor"

Thin slices of fatty beef

Sizzling with green peppers and onions,

To be slathered with Cheese-Wiz

And stuffed in fresh baked hoagie rolls.

A culinary masterpiece.

"World Famous Philadelphia Cheesesteaks,"

A neon sign flashes above the service window,

Below it a piece of cardboard,

With hand-written script pronounces

"English only!"

Two young girls

Clutching handfuls of coins,

Tentatively approach.

The taller girl,

With a long black braid

Raises her index finger,

Softly mouthing

"Uno, por favor."

An employee,

Wearing a grease splattered t-shirt,

Shakes his head,

Conclusively and dismissively,

Mouthing with metered vitriol

"English only!"

The smaller girl,

With two curly pigtails,

Raises her tiny forefinger,

Timorously mouthing "Uno"

As if to clarify their request.

Absent warning,

Or further conversation,

The window is unceremoniously slammed shut,

With the finality of a guillotine,

Leaving the bewildered girls

Alone on the sidewalk

Nervously palpating

Their unspent savings.

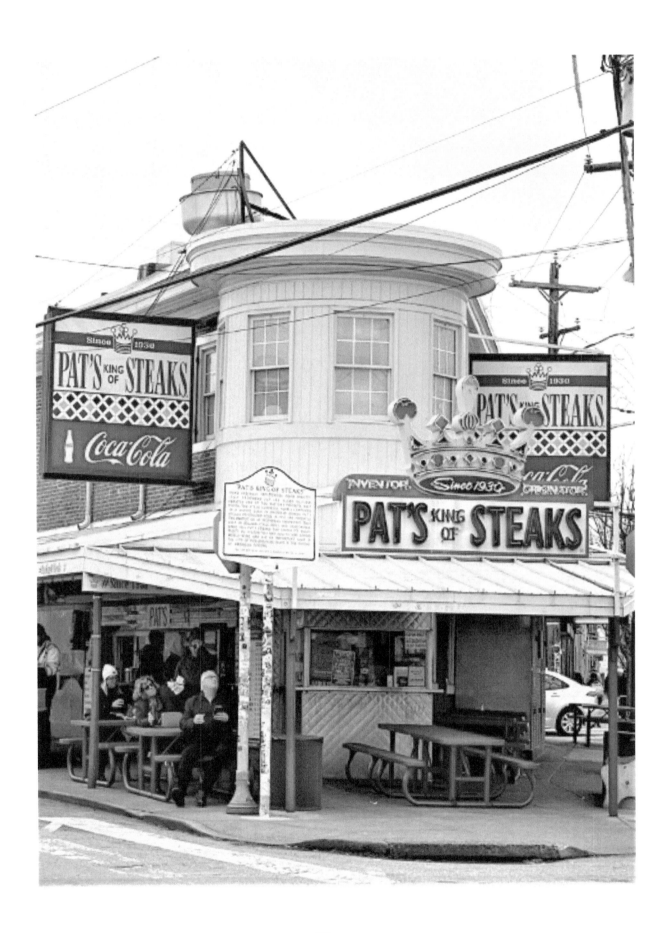

24. Riots in Santiago

The unrest was palpable.

One side of the Maipo River,

The haves,

The other side,

The have-nots.

The majestic light-hued

Granite apartment buildings,

On the have side,

Marred indiscriminately with

Black and red graffiti,

Frenzied eruptions of ire.

On the have-not side,

Dark skinned Chileans

Sit on blankets,

Their make-shift shops,

Selling old platform sandals,

Used electronics,

Anything that might bring in

A couple pesos.

An elderly woman cooks sopaipillas

In a pot of boiling oil,

Balanced on a fire pit,

A pop-up kitchenette

Erected sedulously on the sidewalk,

Emanating an enticing aroma

Of nectarous fried pumpkin and panela.

The fires today are ones of protest,

Not commerce,

Torched buses and delivery wagons,

Flaming metro stations,

The national pride,

Modern transportation,

Up in smoke,

As if bubbling discontent

From the underground,

A Hades of its own making.

The hike in Metro fares,

30 pesos,

Equivalent to four cents,

The boiling point.

Before then,

Everything was just simmering.

But today

Is the day of reckoning,

When the have nots'

Despondent spirits

Are transformed into a blaze of fury,

A rage so perfervid,

That it is inextinguishable by mere,

Desultory protests of graffitied

Palatial walls.

The billionaire President has declared

A state of emergency,

Proclaiming "We are at war!",

As military police

Hose down student remonstrations

With water cannons,

Amidst chants of discontent,

A thunderous turbulence

Which has been brewing,

Churning and percolating

For unsung decades.

25. Crossroads

Forsaking a domicile of security,

Which has evolved into a tent of stagnancy,

He longs to discover unchartered territory,

Far removed from the comfort of familiarity.

Dreams of space travel,

Life on the other planets,

Unexplored galaxies,

New frontiers,

Endless extraterrestrial adventure.

He, the captain of his ship,

Bellowing orders at an eminently qualified,

Yet solicitous, crew…

But wait, he muses…

I have been "relatively happy,"

A reflexive jerk of gilded reminiscence,

Reeling in an already fragile line…

For a sequestered moment…

Taking cautious inventory of his emotions.

But no…

"Relatively happy" is not enough anymore,

Even if it was once enough.

Grasping the brass door handle

With his milky palm,

He turns slowly, deliberately,

As if summoning the precision

Of a venerable, ancestral metronome.

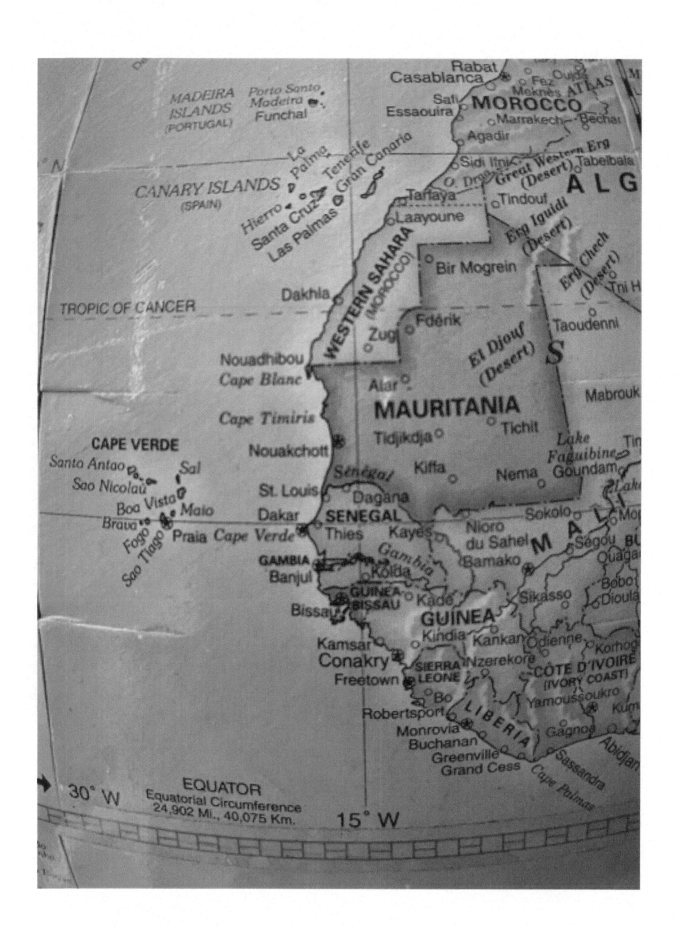

114

26. Exodus from Gambia

As promised, they did escape from Gambia.

However, destination Canary Islands

Was hastily aborted,

With one behemoth surge.

Capsizing off the coast of Mauritania,

Cedar planks of the rickety fishing boat,

Shattered like brittle bones,

Irresolutely projecting arrows of distress

Into the leviathan sea.

83 passengers swam to safety,

While 58 perished,

The fate of the others unknown,

A Pyrrhic victory, at best.

The shivering survivors,

Sit, hunched over,

On a dock at Nouadhibou,

Heads buried in lonesome hands,

Their shock unappeased

By the used towels and plastic water bottles

Distributed by overwrought

And exhausted emergency workers.

With deportation looming,

Dreams vanquished,

And life savings spent,

Asylum in Mauritania,

A country where slavery still flourishes,

Offers little, if any, consolation.

27. Family Vacation

They placate themselves chatting with other passengers,

Drinking Taiwanese beer and exchanging emails,

White knuckles gripping cold aluminum railings

On the upper deck of the grizzled vessel,

As it bobs unceremoniously on turbulent waters.

There was a séance last night on the island

Where they channeled spirits of deceased friends

Wagering their presence in a human circle

As the winds swept audaciously amid the palm trees.

Her mother, both shocked and fascinated,

Found the practice incongruous with Catholicism,

Where the rules are clear and implacable.

As they leave the ship, they hug their new friends,

Promising to share photos,

Yet knowing that they will never see them again.

The rain pours as they maneuver their 1970's Yugo

Through puddles and chasms on route to the airport,

Stopping to buy red wine and sushi,

Which they consume in the car.

On arrival, her father nervously clutches,

The arm rests of the rented wheelchair

As they swiftly commandeer their path

Through crowded hallways and interstices.

The plane is late, they are wet,

Their stomachs unsettled.

Breathing in the thick, humid,

Mildew-laden air at the gate,

They jubilate in the triumph

Of their concerted, perennial,

And unswervingly vigilant effort,

To escape from the ordinary.

28. Harvest

Like an elderly woman giving birth

To bouncing baby boys

From a twisted withered spine,

The ancient gnarled tree

Offers copious fruit every year.

Although appearing fragile,

She is deep-rooted and sturdy,

Unwaveringly dependable.

The farmer remembers his father,

And grandfather picking apples,

His mother and grandmother,

Making pies and conserves,

Auroral September afternoons.

As the deer have already feasted

On the lower hanging pomes,

he agitates the upper limbs

With a long ladder,

Encouraging her,

To give up the fruits of her labor.

When she resists,

He shakes harder,

But not so hard as to injure

Her sinuously contorted limbs.

In time, the fruit begins to fall,

Faster and faster,

With each methodical provocation,

Raining coy,

Blushing,

Apples from the sky,

Landing decorously into the arms

Of soft verdant moss

Blanketing the ground below.

29. Terracotta Warriors, X'ian

Uniquely chiseled features,

Hawkish eyes, prominent chins,

Bespoken lips and countenance,

Assiduously guarding

Emperor Qin's ascent

From the rafters below.

Infantrymen yielding swords,

Dragoons mounted on horseback,

Charioteers lashing whips,

Crossbow-men kneeling erectly,

Each with tales of their own.

Cries to battle, hemorrhagic surges, triumphant subjugations,

Their legacy now eternally blended,

Into astute military defending an empyrean necropolis.

Present but unseen,

Are the faces of seven thousand toiling artisans,

Each also with stories of their own.

Hungry families in mud huts,

Callous, blister-laden hands,

and hot bowls of noodles,

After a long day of molding, firing,

Painting and primping.

Days which were long,

Grow even longer,

With deafening conflagrations,

And sculpted hierarchies,

Merging incandescently

Into a landscape of perpetual deafening silence.

30. The Much-Anticipated Play

The evening is shrouded by a cerulean blue haze.

Having pre-purchased tickets for the much-anticipated play,

We arrive punctually at the theater,

Sinuous, convoluted,

Under construction and in squalid disrepair.

We do the perfunctory bathroom search before the show begins.

No worries, we have lots of time.

You easily find the Men's Room

And go to the bar to get a Peroni.

I cannot find the Ladies Room,

And when I finally unearth one, there is a line,

And only "resting rooms" without toilets.

I keep searching,

Same deal, long lines, only resting rooms.

I finally give up,

Returning to you, with a half full bladder,

Not the way anyone wants to view a play.

You have almost finished your beer,

And are angry because now we are late

for the much-anticipated,

First act.

I decline the last sip

As you half-heartedly

Shove the bottle towards my mouth,

Sardonically spewing to you

That it's all just spit now.

We walk back down the winding corridor,

A combination of the Guggenheim museum,

And Fred Flintstone's house,

But with roseate pink walls,

The color so popular in bathrooms in the 1960's.

When we finally find the auditorium,

We enter from a door at the upper level,

Crestfallen as the play is already in progress.

You don't care,

And insist that we stride,

Down the main aisle,

To our seats towards the front.

I am timorous and refuse.

You insist,

leaving me behind,

Like a deflated balloon,

in the back of the theater,

Where there are only

Yellow plastic benches,

Shoved up against the wall.

As you make your way down the passage,

Our fellow theater goers,

Outraged by your audacity,

Pellet oranges, apples and garbage at you.

I eventually join you between scenes,

Traversing through the darkness.

You are now settled comfortably,

In your maroon velvet throne,

Chatting with your neighbors

Eating stale popcorn.

I settle in beside you,

And have an obstructed view,

To the much-anticipated play.

What I manage to digest of the play,

From behind the column,

Is confusing, poorly written and inordinately over-acted,

a disappointing performance from all perspectives.

At intermission,

The make-shift bar,

set up on a folding banquet table,

amidst the construction,

Is serving plastic flutes of chilled Dom Perignon,

Which we cannot afford.

I continue to search for a functional Ladies Room

While you bitch about the price of the champagne,

And the sordid condition of the theater.

31. Cross Country

Driving her tractor trailer,

Down Route 95, across Route 10,

Up Route 5, and then back along Route 90,

She mused how inter-connected we are,

Physically and spiritually,

Americans on the same journey,

Life, liberty and the pursuit of happiness.

"A curious career choice for a woman,"

Her mother always said,

But this is the land of opportunity,

Where women have equal rights,

And are allowed to drive.

She soaked in the fluid terrain of each state,

While inhaling the intoxicating aroma of diesel,

The scent of unencumbered freedom,

And endless possibilities.

After picking up a load of pharmaceuticals in New York,

She drove across Route 80 to the west coast,

Then back along Route 40 with a haul of oranges.

The middle states,

No less connected than the periphery,

Splashed with mountains and lakes,

Were the heartbeat of the country,

She always believed,

Generating a pulse,

Which pumped oxygen-rich blood,

Throughout the land.

Listening to the impeachment hearings,

This week, while driving,

She conjectured that America had lost its direction,

Needed a roadmap, a reset,

A month off to drive cross-country,

Haul peaches, lemons and auto parts,

Share the wealth,

See the exquisiteness and purity of the land,

That was made for all to share.

After delivering her haul of citrus to North Carolina,

She parked her semi in Flying J's lot,

Tired from the journey,

Crestfallen from the news media,

She bowed her head,

Folded her hands,

And prayed for a braver,

More united,

And markedly more auspicious future,

For the country,

Which at inimitable culmination,

Envelopes and comforts,

Like a soft cotton blanket,

On a crisp autumn evening.

32. Rose

The equanimity of your soulful amber eyes

As present in the warm early autumn breeze

As they were in life,

Reassuring with the perspicacity

Of one who truly knew what mattered,

Intolerant of sanctimoniousness

And pretentiousness,

Yet ever sensitive to fragility

And vulnerability.

The sangfroid with which you bathed

This planet could placate

The most irascible of temperaments

Extirpating the negativity

While honing in on the goodness

Of all who crossed your path.

It is mornings like these

That I seek the pabulum

Of your wisdom, and

The incandescence

Of your spirit,

To guide me through my day.

33. La Serenissma-Un Anno a Venezia

February 2019- Carnevale

Revelers, costumed and masked,

Some stupefying, others staid.

Water taxis skim the canal,

Past Ponte Rialto to Piazza San Marco,

Crowds so dense, Basilica barely visible,

But for the Herculean dome,

Looming over the rapturous masses,

As bacchanalians fold intrinsically into the celebration.

Ubiquitous performers, dancers, musicians,

Courtesans with powdered bouffant hair,

Elaborately brocade silk gowns,

Crimson and gold jackets,

Adorned with alabaster neck scarves,

And chromatic facial guises.

Meandering the parameter,

Across bridges and canals,

Past shops peddling Venetian glass,

Silver jewelry, velvet handbags,

Aperol spritzes with green olives,

Eventually resting, on a warm, sunlit bench,

Perched next to the cool waters of the Adriatic Sea,

Actors in a Fellini film, recharging at intermezzo.

November 2019- Acqua Alta

Sirens' shrill moaning

Bellowing from every port,

Signals an ominous warning

Of six-foot surges,

Crashing onto shore,

Rendering Piazza San Marco

A veritable sea unto itself.

Intrepid tourists

Slosh across wooden boards,

Water seeping menacingly

Into knee-high plastic boots,

While floating suitcases

On top of cresting waves

Manufactured by 35 mph winds.

A shirtless man in goggles,

Rebelliously and defiantly,

Swims lap after lap,

From one end to the other,

Miming and summoning,

An indomitable spirit

Of epic tenacity.

February 2020- Coronavirus

Void of People.

Void of Water.

Only a smattering of rats and pigeons,

Vying for imaginary bread crumbs.

Piazza St. Marco.

A former lyceum,

And swimming hole,

Reduced to a moribund crypt,

Exuding only a thick stench of pestilence.

A few steps away,

As if to render a panacea,

The lapidary canal,

Flows with crystal clear water,

Sparkling like diamonds in sunlight

With gems of fish,

Leaping dolphins,

And graceful swans,

Peacefully skimming,

The lenitive rocking

Of the calm, mellifluous currents.

Caroline Reeves is a Philadelphia lawyer whose love of poetry began while studying English at Cornell University. Her poems are frequently inspired by her passion for travel and commitment to issues of social justice. While not writing poetry, traveling, or practicing law, Caroline enjoys playing corn hole and Scrabble with her husband, Allan, and five sons.

Allan Reeves is a real estate executive whose love of photography began while being dragged along on endless expeditions planned by Caroline. His favorite line, "I'm with her," underplays his prodigious sense of adventure and perspicacious observational skills which create an extraordinary collection of photography.

Made in the USA
Columbia, SC
18 September 2021